Sleeping Rough

Poems by Sylvie Gallimore

and Others

Gale's Publications

First published in 2004 by Gale's Publications

© 2004 Sylvie Gallimore

Produced by
Pomegranate Books, Bristol
www.pomegranatebooks.co.uk
Cover design: John Adler

Printed in Great Britain
by Biddles Ltd, King's Lynn
All rights reserved

No part of this publication may be reproduced, stored in a retrieval system, or transmitted, in any form or by any means, electronic, mechanical photocopying, recording or otherwise, without the prior permission of the publisher and copyright holder

ISBN 0-9548516-0-9

Gale's Publications
Harry Stoke
Bristol BS34 8QH

Dedicated to the Memory of
Justin Lawrence (1973-2003)

and Also to My Friend
Richard (Clive) Beckingham (1951-2004)

About the Author

Sylvie Gallimore was born in Bristol in 1948. She married her husband Richard in 1969 and has three sons and two grandsons.

Sylvie feels privileged to have benefited from a reasonable education, to have friends she can rely on and to have the love of her extended family to fall back on. Her family are the mainstay of her life.

Her eldest son Joseph has been a great influence on the generation of this book. His accepting outlook on life and his wide range of friends have helped Sylvie to gain an insight into the ethnic and cultural mix that this country now embraces and appreciate the depth and richness of its traditions.

Her youngest son Daniel was the actual inspiration for the book, the reasons being made clear in the preface. Her middle son Adam is the reliable steadying influence, whose help with his brother in 1996 and continued love, protection and support ever since, have made writing 'Sleeping Rough' all the more important.

As a supplement to her own poetry, Sylvie runs a firm called Poems to Order (www.poemstoorder.com), where she pens rhymes for celebratory and other events.

Her collection of poems *The Lives and Rhymes of an Ordinary Housewife* was published in the USA by Dorrance in 1994.

Book Contents

Introduction by the Rt Hon David Blunkett MP	11
Author's Preface	13
Foreword	15

Poems:

Sleeping Rough	17
My First Encounter	21
Practical Help	25
Morry	27
Susie	31
Ben	33
Sally	35
Tim	37
Casey	39
Jerry	43
Andrew	45
A Near Thing	47
Mums New Man	49
Simons Gran	51
Mary Pregnant	53
Annie	55
Mandy	57
Those I Left Out	59
My Wishes	63
Noah	65
Scott	67
Buskers	69
No One	71
Chance	73
Full Circle	77
Prison Glue	79
Lost	81
Dangerous Streets	83
When You Left	85
High Rise Blues	87

Introduction

Our country and society has undergone significant changes over the last few decades. Many of these changes have transformed the way we live for the better. There are more people in work, more people are going to university, health care has improved and crime is heading downwards.

There are opportunities for people today that only a decade ago were beyond the reach of the majority of people. Our standard of living and prosperity has never been higher. But for all the progress we have made, considerable challenges remain.

Just as crime and disorder manifests itself in new ways – criminals becoming more organised at trafficking Class A drugs; modern technology used to forge new identities or breach security systems; new threats to our borders and national security – so too does social exclusion.

Where the sight of people sleeping rough was once a common sight in our towns and cities, it is now significantly reduced, and where there were once thousands of families raising their children in bed-and- breakfast accommodation, this is now a thing of the past. The Office of the Deputy Prime Minister has invested considerable resources to bring this about.

But homelessness has become a more complex issue. The lack of a home often masks problems to do with addiction or ill health. To tackle homelessness we must also deal with the reasons why people are homeless – relationship breakdown, debt, drug abuse, unemployment and domestic violence.

This present new challenges for all of us: Government, the voluntary sector, local authorities and homeless people themselves. We need to continue to provide help and support for those that need it. We need to deal with the minority of people who are choosing to live a life of begging and street drinking – causing intimidation and harassment to the law-abiding majority. And we need to continue to clamp down hard on the problems that cause homelessness.

We should be proud of the progress we are making in this country. And we should also remember that there are vulnerable people who continue to need our support, if we are to achieve a society of safety and prosperity for all.

I'm particularly grateful not only to dedicated professionals but to the many volunteers and voluntary organisations up and down the country who are doing such a first class job in giving up their time and care to others.

Rt Hon David Blunkett MP

Author's Preface

In May 1996 my youngest son Daniel suffered an assault in a Bristol Street. He foolishly went to the aid of a young man being attacked and paid a very high price for his bravery. He is now registered blind.

Daniel would be the first to acknowledge that without the support and love of his family his life would be a lot bleaker than it is now. We as a family worked together to get Daniel fit again and able to face the hand that he had been dealt, with dignity. He already had the courage to face anything but initially lacked the strength after weeks on life support.

Years before the assault I had taken an interest in youngsters sleeping rough on the streets but what happened to Daniel made me wonder what the outcome would be if such a person came to grief in the way Daniel had. Family love and support can conquer most things but without it there is no anchor no foundation, no protection. I do not believe a vulnerable homeless person would have survived what Daniel had to fight.

I decided to gather together the now-dusty poems I had written back in 1994/95 and put together a book of poetry, with more recent ones, that would reflect the lives of people who live rough. I hope that if the reader gains a greater insight into how and why these people live such a life, it might give them greater understanding and compassion. The circumstances of our birth are out of our hands. So when you pass someone less fortunate maybe you should think – there but for the grace of God… That could be me.

Sylvie Gallimore

Foreword

I spent a few months talking to youngsters on a regular basis who I saw sleeping rough around the streets of Bristol. This started with an interest in one such young man to whom I spoke almost every weekday for a couple of years. I used to walk to the Clifton Down Shopping Centre in Bristol during my lunch break and every day I bought a pint of milk and a piece of fruit for this young man who could always be seen sitting near the library steps. I didn't want to give money since I wasn't sure what it would be spent on. I wanted to see that at least he had a bit of calcium and some vitamins in his diet, so I didn't give him the choice. I suppose it's the mother hen syndrome that so many of us suffer from, and no one more than me.

He seemed a nice enough lad, in his early 20s, tall with a fine face and pleasant speaking voice. I imagined that he could have got a job and set up a home quite easily. The reasons why he hadn't follow this path fascinated me, and I got to hear his story slowly over several months. This then got me interested in why other youngsters might find themselves sleeping rough, so I decided to ask a few.

I discovered that the reason people have left home are varied – some sad, some foolhardy. But just talking to these people gave me a far better understanding of why some youngsters find themselves without hope and without a home. I rather hope that as you read my stories you might see beyond the outstretched hand and into the hearts and minds of some of those homeless souls out there. I know that every time I get into my bed I am thankful that I have a warm and clean home and that my children are all safe with a roof over their heads. I also spare a moment to think about those who are less fortunate. I hope after you have read this book you will do the same.

Sylvie Gallimore

Sleeping Rough

I wanted to question youngsters
Who slept rough on the street,
I wanted to know what drove them there
And if they had enough to eat.
I wanted to listen to what they said
And try to understand
So I sought them out one cold wet morn
With notebook clutched in hand.

Not once did I consider that
This task be fraught with danger
Though I was going, God knows where?
To converse with a stranger.
I didn't go empty handed,
I took milk and bread and cheese
Bones for the dog and blankets.
I really tried to please.

I need the inside story,
What makes these youngsters tick?
It's all very well while healthy,
But what happens when they're sick?
Do they ever see there parents,
Did they leave of their free will?
Do they go home for a visit,
Are they cared for when they're ill?

What about the dentist,
Do they leave their teeth to crumble?
How do they cope on a winters night
When their stomachs start to rumble?
They can't just open up the fridge
And take out tasty snacks
They just lay awake still hungry,
With the wind upon their backs.

I just simply can't imagine
The sort of lives they lead,

Tucked up here in my cosy bed
With another good book to read.
I'm surrounded by warmth
And people who care,
The children I love
And the life that we share.

I look at my chicks
Tucked up safe in our nest,
But my mind keeps returning
To all of the rest
Of those youngsters out there
In the cold, and I must,
Go seek out their stories,
Once I've gained their trust.

S G

The following pages relate what occurred,
Stories told to a stranger, "twas sad what I heard.
They might not be true, but they're as told to me
They could be fact, or just pure fantasy.

My First Encounter *(Cotham, Bristol, 1994)*

I saw him nearly every single day
Sat in a heap when I passed that way.
Then one day my curiosity
Began to get the best of me.
I had to know, I needed to know,
What made him tick what laid him low.

When you live in comfort it's hard to see
How someone would choose to live as he.
Or maybe it's not a matter of choosing
More of a matter of winning or losing.
I decided I needed to understand why
He chose to live outside, under the sky.

I worried about toothache and chill.
Who took care of him if he became ill?
My kids I'd tuck up in bed with a smile
And nurse them to health after a while
But he exposed to weather and damp
Would shiver alone in his home made camp.

It didn't seem right and didn't seem fair
That youngsters should sleep in the cold night air.
Where are his parents? Are they alive or dead?
Do they care where he is and is hungry or fed?
Or was he simply a rebellious lad
Who wasn't content with the life that he had?

At last I approach the subject with care
And he in turn laid his life quite bare
He told of foster homes that didn't work out
Of bullying adults who only could shout.
Of people who should never have had
A dog let alone a vulnerable lad

Of those who took money to look after a kid
But couldn't wait for the moment when they could get rid
Of that tedious child with demanding ways
That you have to have because it pays.

People that give the minimum care
And would much rather that you were never there.

Sometimes it worked and the people were good
They listened with care and understood.
Just as life became settled along came the men
Who wanted to send you away again.
Back to your parents who had lost the plot
But your family allowance could buy more pot.

These people demand that the child chooses
Between carers that care and dad that abuses.
No contest you'd think but blood ties are strong
So you choose the parents knowing you're wrong.
Everything's geared to return you to these
Inadequate people that you're anxious to please.

You knew that quite soon they would find it wearing
That they had a child and would again stop caring.
So you go to school and you smell and kids jeer.
You hide in the corner and shed a tear
But nothing changes, it doesn't seem fair.
You've drawn the short straw and they just don't care.

And so it goes on year after years.
Your childhood dissolves in a floods of tears.
You long for the time you can start anew
On your own feet, but choices are few.
No parental advice of which to follow
Just lonely despair in which to wallow.

No grandmas to run to and uncles that care
No siblings to cling to with stories to share.
A lonely child, now a lonely man
Getting by as best I can.
And my best ain't too good as you can see
That is why I'm here and will always be.

A job, don't be silly, I've no papers to show
That I went to school, so who'd want to know.

I didn't stay long in each home or school
On the surface you'd think me an ignorant fool.
I'm street wise you know and have proved that I can
Look after myself as both child and a man.

                                        SG

Practical Help.

I gave him milk and fruit to sustain him
I'm sure he'd rather have the money
And who would blame him.

I wanted to be sure that he was at least fed
And not on drugs and booze
Right out of his head.

So I don't give money only practical aid
Not cigarettes either,
Just milk, fruit and bread I'm afraid.

SG

Morry *(Cotham, Bristol 1994)*

He looked slightly mongol
But I might have been wrong.
He looked fairly tidy
But smelt very strong.
His name was Morry,
What sort of a name is that?
It's a name I might have used
But only for my cat!

He laughed when I said that,
It really broke the ice.
We talked and he scratched
I think that he had lice.
He put his cap upon my head
And laughed as he spoke
I took lice home that day
And that isn't a joke.

He behaved like a child.
I felt he would never survive
A winter in the open.
The others would eat him alive.
He might be saved by good humour
An endearing trait.
But was I prepared to leave him
To his fate?

I was not sure of the options
I had at that time.
He was nothing to me,
But it felt like a crime
To walk away
No backward glances
Leaving this lad
To take his chances.

I spoke to another young man
Sitting near.

I told him Morry was different
And why I did fear
For this vulnerable child
In a grown man's frame
Who thought every thing
Was only a game?

                S G

The Bearpit at Broadmead in Bristol was the home to an extended family of homeless people for many years.

In 1995 I spent a great deal of time talking to several of these rough sleepers, gathering their stories and putting them into a poetry format to form the basis of this book.

Susie (*the softy's*) Story

Susie was the one, that I worried most about
She had a gentle way with her, I never heard her shout
She hated being dirty, and took a lot of care
Went to the swimming baths, just to wash her hair.
She kept herself together, trying to look neat
Not an easy task, when living on the street.

She wouldn't tell her story, a family row I'd say
I hoped she'd have the courage, to phone her mum one day.
I used to take her sandwiches, the birds all got a share.
She was a pretty little thing, with wavy mousy hair.
She always looked so out of place, much too clean by half
The type of girl that can't survive without a daily bath.

One day when Susie looked rather peaky
I decided to do something rather sneaky.
Visit the Sally Army with all that I knew
about young Susie, and see what could they do?
Well, they did it, and Mum appeared in the rain
Lots of tears, then she took her home again.

S G

Ben *(the deserter's)* Story

I was in the army, I couldn't stand the pace
All those jumped up ponces getting in my face.
Do this, do that, whatever, it was a real bad trip
They said I had a problem and that was too much lip.
I decked a big instructor, boy was that a bad mistake
Awaiting a court-martial was when I made the break.

They say the army takes young boys and turns them into men
I believed that once, but now is now, and brother, that was then.
It gives a group of morons a chance to be real tough
You get pushed right to the limits, and I had had enough
I swung with a left, landing square on the jaw
Of the biggest, meanest sergeant, the sod of them all.

I had no choice but run, I had to get away
I had no place to go, but still I couldn't stay.
The army trained me well, in the art of sleeping rough
Compared to the barracks, this life ain't so tough.
I'll not stay too long, I've got a plan
To get far away, as soon as ever I can.

S G

Sally's Story

Can you spare me some of your change I cry
To the shoppers and walkers passing me by
As I sit curled up in my usual spot
On a dirty blanket be it wet, cold or hot.

The police come to move me on and I moan
As I wrap in my blanket, all that I own.
Sometimes I wonder if home was so bad
When I remember the bedroom that once I had.

I won't return to my father, of that you can be sure
For I was just his daughter, but he wanted so much more
Mother left, he said, "You will replace her totally"
When I grasped just what he meant, I simply had to flee.

So here I am, a lonely soul, barely out of school
I never would have guessed that life could be so cruel.
As I sit here on the pavement, my mind is full of hate
Why did Mother leave me, she must have guessed my fate.

S G

Tim's Story

I met a group of strangers, they all lived in a squat.
We put all we had together, we didn't have a lot.
They had two old dogs, each played their part
Their soulful eyes, touched the hardest heart.
How come people walk past young men,
Without a backward stare?
If sitting with a tatty old dog, they suddenly seem to care!

This isn't how I planned my life and isn't how I'll end it
I will rejoin the world one day, but 'til then I'll just sit
Here on the ground a begging, with dog, and cap in hand
Sharing all I get each day, with that dirty like wise band
Of life's forgotten youngsters, for whom no one gives a toss
No one giving orders, we're all equal, there's no boss.

Of course there's no one there to offer, any good advice
We're just a group of losers left to our own device.
We seem to have an inner strength, which means we will survive.
We are not unlike primeval man, from which we did derive.
Living on our wits and dodging inclement weather
Like a real primitive tribe, who hunt and live together.

I live a life, not wrapped in rules, I live a life that's free
So don't go home a thinking you, should feel sad for me.
I'm fine, I'm only young, I won't stay here for ever
I won't always be a loser, I feel I'm much too clever
I still have dreams, I still have hopes, I'm not an empty shell.
My dreams and hopes might come about, only time will tell.

At the moment I'm quite happy, I live from day to day
I don't want much and like to live, in this simple way.
If I start to feel it's boring, that's when
I'll re think my life, but not until then.
I do no harm, I don't do drugs, or steal
I beg for just enough, for a drink and wholesome meal.

                                                    S G

Casey *(the rebel's story)*

I'm inclined to pop pills and I do smoke hash
I've a stud in my nose, it doesn't make me trash.
I'm afraid my father somehow didn't agree
And I became, unacceptable to my family.
They can go jump, I don't care a jot
I can sit here unbothered, smoking pot.
I can tell that you think it's a waste, well tough
But at the moment I love to be sleeping rough.

A guy gave me a bed once, he said "pay in kind"
Didn't take much to figure what was on his mind.
Still it was easy money, it makes no odds to me
Now I tout myself about, and do it regularly
I can make more in an hour, than a week on the street
What the hell, at least, it gets me off my feet.

I don't do it in doorways, or alleys or the like
Anyone with that in mind can go and take a hike.
I like a little comfort if I'm gonna risk my life,
What with AIDS and Hepatitis, that's a lot of strife!
No show without a safety net, they have to use a rubber
Or I don't perform, as simple as that, they can find another scrubber.

A while ago I found a pal and we worked as a pair
We had a lot of takers and everything we'd share.
She was fun, just like the sister, that I never had,
One day, she simply disappeared, for a while I felt quite sad.
We didn't know where she came from, so we couldn't check and see.
Why she left, or where she went and was it willingly?

Don't look like that, what's it to you, you didn't even know her.
She was just another piece of trash, lying in the gutter
She'll be alright, I bet she's gone and shacked up with a trick,
Either that, or they've got her, down in the local nick.
Either way she'll survive, she's street wise that's for sure
Even if she's gone back home, she'll soon be back for more.

Alright, so you think I'm too hard, that might be true
But she's gone now, that's tough, so what's it to you?
Except now there's one less story to hoard
One less sad pathetic tale, for you to record.
Is that your angle, is that your fear?
You missed out on a beaut of a story to hear?

S G

Jerry (*the one I couldn't handle*)

There was one filthy looking lad,
I couldn't believe how much he stunk.
His language was disgusting,
And he was always drunk.
I could understand why he was there
No one would take him in,
He was the sort of boy who thought
Politeness was a sin.

Hard to think, he was probably once
his mother's pride and joy.
If she saw him now, she'd not believe
He's her little baby boy.
He made an art form out of burping,
You'd have to be there to hear
Jerry in full volume
It must be all that gassy beer.

He really was disgusting
I couldn't make myself believe,
That he wasn't putting on an act,
Or am I just naive.
I never thought that people
Could behave in such a way
Lay about, just lost in drink
Every single day.

What's the point, I ask myself
You might as well be dead
As spend your life forever
Completely out your head.
But Jerry seemed to disagree
This was the life he craved.
It seemed to him acceptable
The way that he behaved.

He didn't care a dam for anyone,
Of this you can be sure

Couldn't hold a conversation,
He simply drank and swore.
He frightened people passing by
Who might have helped him out
If they didn't give him money
He would simply swear and shout.

He got arrested several times
He didn't seem to care
I bet they didn't search him
I bet they didn't dare.
They wouldn't want to touch his clothes
Just lock him up 'til morning.
Then quickly send him on his way
With yet another warning.

I never stood too close to him
I could stand to see,
All those nose studs that he had,
What does he want to be?
Bulls have rings put in their noses
To lead the things about.
But why would humans chose to look
Like such a scruffy lout.

I never caught his age,
He looks around the twenties.
It's rather hard to tell
As he sits there with his empties.
His features, if he washed,
Would be actually quite strong.
He wouldn't be so bad
If he could get rid of that pong.

You don't expect to be too neat
If your sleeping rough.
And I realise that it has to help,
You live if you're quite tough.
But there's tough, and plain disgusting
And Jerry was the latter.

And the saddest part was that he thought
It really didn't matter.

I couldn't stand too near to him,
Didn't want to breath his air.
I'm sure you'd catch some bug from him
If you didn't take good care.
The air went blue each time he spoke
It wasn't from the reefer smoke.
He struggles to find enough cash for dope
Though he always said that he was broke!

S G

Andrew's Story

I was shacked up with this girl, we had a baby son
We were barely seventeen and should be having fun
Pressure mounted, bills came in, I knew I couldn't cope
Instead of paying bills, I lost myself in dope.
She couldn't stand the worry and went home to her clan
I packed my bags as well and sought out my old man.
He didn't want to know, he'd warned me at the start
Still I rather hoped he might have had a change of heart.

A heart that cold don't change, I had to turn around
There was no going back, a new life must be found.
My mum had died when I was young, our family just sank,
My sister ran away from home, and the old man, he just drank.
Looked for work, none was there, is there no hope for me
Is a cardboard box on a pavement floor, all that I can see.
Some would say the fault is mine, up to a point 'tis true
I was young and foolish needing help to pull me through.

I reckon if my mum had lived I'd sing a different tune
As it is, the life I lead, I think I'll join her soon.
There doesn't seem much point, in trying any more
Destiny has plans for me, I'll stay the lowly poor.
I don't blame my dad, he has his own life to lead
I never should have helped produce, another mouth to feed.
I had trouble feeding just myself, the baby had no chance
And that poor girl I lived with, I led her quite a dance!

I've probably got, just what I deserve, after all I am self taught
In the ways of being a waster, and amounting up to nought.
If I sit a begging all the day, until my pocket's lined
Then I'll just search all the night, a dealer so to find.
I won't spend it on food, or a bed for the night
I never do nothing that could be deemed right
It don't worry me, that my son, might come to seek me out
I know that I'll be dead and gone, before that comes about.

S G

A Near Thing

Skipped school at fifteen, an addict soon after.
On a down wards spire without much laughter.
The habit is costly and I never will share
Needles with no one, I just wouldn't dare.

I'm nineteen now, quite an old hand I'm sure.
Four years now since I walked out the door.
I was nagged at home and bullied at school
Then one day I just lost my cool.

I picked up a knife I don't know to this day
If I would have stuck anyone in my way.
But they all stood aside and let me pass by
I was glad none of my kin had to die.

I doubt that I would have done it at all
But I tell you it was a very close call.
I was shaking with rage and there was the knife.
In a moment I could have taken a life.

I wasn't even on drugs back then.
I'd never want that to happen again.
It frightened the hell out of me to be sure.
I'm just glad they let me out of that door.

No one tried to restrain me or follow me out
No one asked me what it was all about.
They just looked glad to see the back of me
I dropped the knife and out did flee.

If my dad had been in I think I'd be dead
I threatened my mum and my sisters instead.
My little brother too, they all were there.
The cat was sitting at the foot of the stair.

Quite a homely picture I spoilt that day
When I lost the plot and ran away.
I can't even remember what started the strife
Or even where I got the knife.

I think it might have begun at school
I seemed to get stressed there as a rule.
I wanted to leave, lessons were tough
The bullies always treated me rough.

Still no reason to wonder four years on
If they're all relieved that I have gone.
I wonder how mother related the story.
I certainly left in a blaze of glory.

                        S G

Mum's New Man

I guess you've heard this same old chestnut,
Mother brought home a new man.
We didn't get on so I had to leave,
We had a terrible row and I ran.
I should have planned things better,
I was in the last year of school
I know I should have waited,
I know I've been a bit of a fool.
But when you're only fifteen,
You don't reason all that well
You just think things are as bad as they get,
So then, what the hell!

You think things can't get worse, you're wrong,
Rock bottoms still to come.
You're on the streets, too young to work,
Hungry, crying for your mum.
But she won't appear, she's busy now,
Starting her life anew
A new life with a new man,
Long term plans do not include you.
For a while you think the police will come
To march you straight back home.
After a month or so you guess
That you are really on your own.

Was I that hard to live with?
Until 'he' came I would have said no.
My mum and I made a pretty good team,
'Til she found herself a beau.
He isn't even nice to her,
He forever throws his weight about.
My Dad had been so kind,
Why would she now want such a lout?
Her choice I suppose, but he isn't mine
And I could take the strain.
I could stay at home and close my eyes,
Or live out in the rain.

He hit her hard, still the choice was hers,
She could have thrown him out.
Then he hit me, and that was that,
I was out of there - no doubt!
Still I suppose I should have waited,
Mum might have come around.
Regained her pride, stood up for me,
And together stood our ground.
I was too scared to wait,
Of this towering hell of a man.
I stayed in my room and cried for hours
Then finally I ran.

Now I don't have a room, just a blanket,
And cold floor for a bed
But at least I'm not scared any more,
Except that I might not be fed.
Usually some one will toss me a coin,
Enough for a bite to eat,
A cup of tea or coffee,
And for a moment I get a warm seat,
In the local greasy spoon.
It's the only place, I feel I am welcome.
I tell the lady there what happened to me,
And all about my mum.

                                    S G

Simon's Gran

I often wonder if my Gran has asked where I might be
And If I would be welcome there, I'm just to scared to see.
If she rejects me too, I've no more hopes to keep.
She might just be my saviour, I felt our bond was deep.

When I was young I always spent my spare time with my Gran.
She always was so proud of me, she was my biggest fan.
She made me feel I could do no wrong, she always took my part
And for that she'll hold a special place forever in my heart.

I fell out with my father, because I couldn't get a job
He said I was becoming a lazy useless yob.
It's not my fault, the jobs aren't there, it isn't an excuse
But every day I came home to the same verbal abuse.

Each day became a battle, it was impossible to stay
So I packed a bag, toothbrush and comb, and left one summers day
I hadn't thought about the winter, 'cos it seemed a long way on
Then suddenly the autumn came and warm nights had all gone.

It was fun under the stars when warm, then the winter came
And living rough with a bunch of mates ceased to be a game.
Now we're talking survival, fighting chesty coughs and flu
I'm going to see my Gran, she'll know just what to do.

I've had enough, I stayed a while, I guess I'm just too soft
But I want hot meals inside me and my room back in the loft.
I'll even face my father's scorn and tell him he was right
If in turn I get a bite to eat and a warm bed every night.

But first I'll try my Gran, with her my greatest hopes lay.
She'll greet me with an outstretched arm and tell me I can stay.
And if this happens in the way that I really hope it might
My Gran will be my saviour, I'll be rescued from my plight.

S G

Mary – Pregnant and Unloved

When I first knew I was pregnant, I thought, what the hell
There's no stigma any more, so my mum I've got to tell.
The air went blue, "What have you done, you useless stupid brat,
You've made your bed now lie in it, you're out", and that was that!
I was out in the street with just my clothes and moved into a squat.
My clothes got pinched and I got sick, ending up in a hospital cot.

I lost the child, I guess it was best, I couldn't look after myself
A social worker helped me, to get back to full health.
She got in touch with mum, who said I could go home again now,
As if after that, I'd spend a day, under the roof of that selfish cow!
I'd had got a council place if the baby had been born
Instead I sleep in doorways, alone to dream and mourn.

I've lost interest in life, I sell myself for a drink and a fag
I'm twenty three but look more like a forty year old hag.
Sleeping rough and eating meals you've fetched out of the bin
Don't do a lot for pearly teeth and plays havoc with your skin
I probably need glasses but I don't get a lot to read
So I suppose it isn't on the list of things I really need.

I think I'll live and die this life, it's been six year to date
And I've only got myself to blame for getting in this state.
To be honest though, I like this life, not every part it's true.
I miss bubbly baths, clean white sheets and soft paper in the loo.
I don't miss my mum, she had her chance, and let me down real bad.
And I still dream about the baby and sometimes of it's Dad.

I suppose I should have told him, though it's a little late to say
I don't think he would have helped me, I guess he would have walked away
He was married and so much older, with quite a lot to loose
So what the heck, why tell him, he would only have had to choose.
And it wouldn't have been me, his lifestyle didn't allow
For a bit of rough on the side, no, he would ran and how!

So I would have added another rejection to join the rest
I think the choice to go it alone was probably the best.

Best for me at least, but not for babe, of course, it died,
If I told you that I'm glad of that, I think you'd know I lied.
I've started to rely on drugs, so things can't get much worse
To think that when I was a child, I wanted to be a nurse.

I wanted to be a lot of things, but never to be like this
A pop star or a model, but a tramp - I'll give that a miss.
Life doesn't always go as planned and it's easy now to see
How simply I slip down this past, there's no one to blame but me.
For a while I blamed my mother, she could have helped me through
The pregnancy and aftercare, but this she didn't want to do.

I wonder if she thinks of me, and of my stillborn son
Does she feel a little guilty about the death of the little one.
After all he was her grandchild, the only one she'd own
Yet she chose to just reject me to face all that grief alone.
I was an only child, and no man would want me now
So she'll never have another one, the silly selfish cow.

I'm starting to get maudlin now, over memories long past
I think I need another score, to wipe them out at last.
But as the kick wears off each time I feel I'm deeper down
Along the path of misery, only drugs or booze can drown.
Perhaps if you could tell my tale, others would take heed
And instead of giving up they might seek out the help they need.

S G

Annie's Story

Mother said 'she wanted to find herself'
I didn't know she was lost!
She said she needed her own space
And then she told me the cost.
She had brought up us kids, now she found,
We were breathing in her air.
She wanted to live the next few years
Without so much as a care.

I think I was thick, I found it hard to grasp,
Exactly where this led
The fact she was trying to chuck me out
Never came into my head.
Some sort of middle-age crisis
Had suddenly taken hold.
And where the hell did that leave me,
Suddenly out in the cold.

So 'she wanted to find herself'
And I was cramping her style.
I was the last one left at home,
I wanted to stay a while.
But there wasn't very much else
I really felt I could say.
I'd have to go I suppose,
If she felt I was in the way.

At first I stayed with my sister
But her husband made me ill.
He kept making rude suggestions
And asked, if I was on the pill.
It didn't seem too wise to stay
Around that man too long.
I felt I was in danger, tho' I guess
I could have been wrong.

So then I stayed with my brother,
At first things went well.

Tho' each evening I sat with
The nephews from hell!
I clean the house and ironed the clothes
I really didn't mind
'Til they started to go out most nights
Always leaving me behind.

I was only seventeen
And needed to have some fun,
But if I moaned I was always told
I was the selfish one.
I knew people who lived in a squat,
In the day they begged on the street.
To one as naive as me,
This life style sounded neat.

So I thought I'd give it a whirl
It was surely worth a try.
At the moment I find it exciting,
It might change as time goes by.
I sit and play the flute,
Those lessons were really worth while.
So although, strictly speaking I beg,
At least I do it with style.

                                              S G

Mandy *(the nanny)*

I was a live-in nanny, to a couple down in Poole
I wasn't qualified on paper, but they said 'OK that's cool'
We'll have to pay you cash in hand, but not the going rate
It all seemed fair enough to me, I didn't guess my fate.

The guy was a friend of my fathers, so how could I lose out?
He turned out to be a ladies man, who knocked his wife about.
I expect you've guessed what happened next, he went and tried it on.
I told his wife, who yelled and screamed, the next day I was gone.

He phoned my dad and told him that I'd tried to spoil his life,
By telling wild false stories about him to his wife.
I told my dad how he beat her up, he didn't believe a word
How could it be true, he was dad's old mate, so it couldn't have occurred?

My father wouldn't forgive me, he said I had let him down
My choice seemed to be, confess I lied, or get right out of town.
I decided to choose the latter, I was after all in the right
So I packed my bags, kissed my mum, and left for good that night.

So that's how I came to be here, amongst this merry band
Of dropouts and forgotten folk who need a helping hand.
The 'useless lumps' and 'scruffy yobs' who clutter up the street
Have turned out to be the very best friends I feel I'll ever meet.

We share everything, food, drink and clothes, and even body heat
In the throws of winter, when forced to sleep on the street.
As a rule we manage to squat a while, until they turf us out
And we always stick together, of that you can have no doubt.

Our trust is in each other, not 'look out for number one'
We are more like the Musketeers, than an single shooting gun.
There is a safety felt in numbers and a kind of family feeling
We all came here on a mission, with wounded souls for healing.

Together I think we'll make it, though it is still early days
We hope some day to find a home, I'm sure there must be ways.
We're not on drugs, not strong on booze, we are a bit of a cult.
Determined all to stay quite clean, and getting a good result.

So we're a strong little band, all life's rejects, it's true
And it's hard to explain to people like you.
But we still have some pride and a long-term plan
We find strength in each other, right to a man.

S G

Those I Left Out

There were a few stories
I couldn't relate
Those too drunk or too high
To communicate.

Those worn out and tired,
Too hard and too cold.
Those battered and bruised,
Too wrecked and too old.

Those physically spent
And mentally scarred.
Those that self harm
Shattered and marred.

Old timers, long livers
Duckers and divers
Thieves and hard men
Violent skivers.

No-hopers no planners
No brain cells intact
Just drugged up and drunk
No future in fact.

S G

My Wishes

Finding them young is the secret
Getting them off of the street
Give them a feeling of self worth
Getting them back on their feet.

Getting them help and assistance
A bath and clean clothes to wear
Giving them hope to move on
Giving them shelter and care

Giving them motivation.
Healing the scars of their past
Giving them reasons to live
Giving them hope at last.

Giving them help to drop drugs
Giving them help to get clean
Give them the will to look forwards
Not to look back where they've been.

S G

Summary of the 1995 Poems

There were several more rough sleepers who I could have approached but chose not to. I felt they might not have been very responsive or forthcoming so I picked the easier targets. Some stories I chose not to use at all.

So the section you have just read is a cross-section of the homeless people out there at that time. I hope some of their stories touch a chord.

The next section is from 2000 onwards.

Noah

Not all start life on the streets in their teens.
Some are latecomers, which is stranger it seems.
Some have had jobs and homes of their own
Some have had children, not quite fully grown.

I remember when Noah was a father of three
At school concerts and fetes he always would be.
He once did fatherly things like kicking balls in the park
Went on picnics and swam before life became dark.

Noah was once a regular guy
A wife three kids and a mortgage so why
Did he pack in his job and get scared of life?
Was it pressure that came with kids and a wife?

So why did he flip and have regular rages?
When did push became thump and go on for ages?
Simple things happened like not wanting a bath.
What made his mind slip from the regular path?

Medical help the wife tried to seek,
She hoped she could get him back on his feet.
But Noah wouldn't go, so life became tough.
This once loving husband kept cutting up rough

The police got involved it wasn't her choice.
Neighbours noticed the tone of his raised voice.
They could hear through the wall and telltale mark,
Bumps, bruises and cuts as his mind became dark.

He needed help but prison did loom
If he didn't lift his aim and end this gloom.
Instead of helping himself with medical care
He packed his bags and ran out of there.

Now he lives on the streets like a loser in life
When he once had it all, a good home and wife.
He didn't look back, he never returned.
Respect of his kids now lost, bridges burned.

How strange when they see him out in the street
A scruffy hobo who once was so neat

They cross the road and pretend he's not there
And he stands head bowed and can only stare.
Does he regret the pain he has put others through
Or does he see it as something he just had to do?

Was his sanity at risk if he stayed in his home?
Was his sanity saved by this life on the roam?
All these questions and more I have wanted to know
But can't get him to talk about times long ago.

Now his wife has a partner and he's still on his own
His past life forgotten, his children now grown.

S G

Scott

When rushing home from town quite late
I saw a youngster with a begging plate.
He looked barely sixteen, not worldly like some
I thought 'God, he should be at home with his mum.'

Walking through the underpass, avoiding the rain
I saw the same youngster curled up again.
This time I found it too hard to pass by
I thought of my own sons and wanted to cry.

I went to the kiosk and purchased some food
Ask if I could join him, at first he was rude.
Of course he was scared, he didn't know me.
I could have been from the powers that be.

I persisted until I was told to sit down.
He accepted the food with a nod and a frown.
I could tell by the speed that he ate the roll
That sleeping rough was taking it's toll.

He was new on the streets of this I was sure
Though his hands were black and looked quite sore.
I imagined him crying himself to sleep
His eyes so red, sitting there in a heap.

His eyes told me his situation was grave
His skin so soft, he was too young to shave.
I asked where he came from, he wasn't sure
Why I wanted to know, were my motives pure?

I told him about my sons and my life
In return he said little about his own strife.
I wanted to know if he'd run away
Did he mean to return back home one day?

He took some coaxing but I wore him down
He opened up but still with that frown.
He wasn't sure what to make of me.
Did I really care, why would that be?

I told him about my own son and how
He had lost his sight defusing a row.
He was really sorry for my son's plight
But thought it was foolish to break up a fight.

He said he saw fights everyday in the street
And he always beat a hasty retreat.
Don't get involved it's safer that way
Then you'll be in one piece at the end of the day.

I tried to encourage the boy to go home
Why make life tough if you don't have to roam.
He'd had a row with his parents 'tis true
I felt going home was the right thing to do.

I looked for Scott on my way home next day.
He wasn't around, did I scare him away?
I hope he went home, he said he might
Go home and make up for the family fight.

I could imagine the pain that I would feel.
The pain of losing a child would never heal.
I know we're not all the same, why would we be?
But surely most mothers would feel like me.

Lots of youngsters out there run away on a whim
But it's a jungle out there, it's sink or swim.
There are people that care and places to go
Projects like Shelter will help when you're low.

S G

Buskers

Sitting cross-legged with dog and guitar
To sing for your supper seems quite bizarre.
Strumming away, the tunes gentle flow
On the summer's breeze to and fro.

No one seems to mind if buskers play on
They seem to enjoy the drifting song.
Some are so clever I'm often amazed
By the hidden talent that hunger displays.

Penny whistles ring out a lively dance
And lift a few spirits maybe perchance.
Dogs always look tired but prick up one ear
When the coins drop in the hat that's near.

There is one on the fiddle and one on the flute
I pass them each day on my usual route.
Clever girls who I doubted slept rough
They don't actually look that tough.

Buskers aren't always homeless you know
They're just making a living from fiddle and bow.
I questioned these girls and they live in a squat
An empty house that was left to rot.

They didn't want a conventional life.
No intention of being both mother and wife.
Free as birds until the money stops flowing.
Then they'll think again about where they are going.

They visit relations, mum knows where they are.
Life's an adventure, or it has been so far.
They live with friends and are eager to stay.
If the novelty wanes they'll go home one day.

Extra music tuition proved useful it's true.
Not quite how their parents expected it to.
They were nice girls, just enjoying each day
Singing for their supper in the usual way.

No One

No one to help us
No one to guide us
No one to feed us
No one to hide us
No one to watch us
No one to see us
No one to want us
No one to free us.

No one to care for
No one to try for
No one to hope for
No one to die for
No one to wish for
No one to look for
No one to clean for
No one to cook for.

No one to plan with
No one to wake with
No one to grow with
No one to break with
No one to read with
No one to think with
No one of importance
But plenty to drink with.

S G

Chance

Is our life determined by the throw of a dice?
Do you pick the short straw and that leads to vice?
Is our history written before we are even born?
Or do we shape it ourselves, on this I am torn?

I believe your luck starts with your status at birth.
We can't choose for ourselves where we're born on this earth.
The haves and have-nots you can tell at a glance,
So it hardly seems fair that so much is just chance.

S G

Full Circle

When I was baby
To my blanket I was stuck.
I dragged it everywhere with me
I thought it brought me luck.

In pram and then in push chair
Each day we'd to the shop
And I clung on to that blanket
Until to sleep I'd drop.

My mother couldn't part me
From that tatty piece of cloth
And if she even tried
She'd surely feel my wrath.

And now I'm that much older
And yet things remain the same
I still cling to a blanket
It's all I have to my name.

It's my warmth my bed my cover
My shelter my tent my home.
Others try to steal it
Because they've lost their own.

So life has gone full circle
Please don't let that be all
I have to hope for in my life
My back's against the wall.

Daniel Gallimore

A Special Contribution

    I worked voluntarily in Horfield Prison for 18 years – leaving some time ago. Whilst there I realised that there is a link between homelessness and lawlessness. There is a financial draught between the age of 16 and 18 which could easily drive youngsters into the world of crime. Obviously drugs also play a big factor as well. If a youngster is out there on the streets for whatever reason he or she has to eat and food has to be paid for. It is not always as simple as one would hope to stay on the straight and narrow if there is no family support.

    I have enlisted the help of inmates at Horfield Prison and they kindly allowed me to include a selection of poems in this book 'straight from the horses mouth' so to speak. They speak volumes.

Prison Glue

Stuck in this place with nothing to do
Stuck down so tight with invisible glue
Stuck down so tight with nothing to gain
Only our hopes and dreams of bail again.
To return to court you might stand a chance
If you have a bad day apply for enhanced.
The pain it hurts it cuts like a knife
With no one to blame it's a glitch in our life.
For I hope it's possible to stay out of strife
Who wants to be a prisoner serving life?
When I get out I must stay off the booze
But you say to yourself I've nothing to loose.
One night of madness and you know it's bad news,
You wake up in the gutter with the morning dews.
You try to get up but you're flat on your back
Saying to yourself why did I mix booze with crack
With a blink of an eye you will be straight back.
In prison I mean with nothing to do
Stuck down so tight with invisible glue.

Jamie

Lost

Life for me is a struggle
Of constant ups and down
Forever trying to find my way
But just going round and round.

Drugs and crime and loneliness
Don't copy me, my life's a mess.
I'm praying for the help I need
Don't follow me, I'm not in the lead

                                        Anon

Dangerous Streets

Just when you think life can't get no worse
You wake up in the gutter
Stomped and kicked and bashed about
By a homicidal nutter.

You'd think if you ain't got nothing
There's nothing they could take.
But they have to show their power
They can't give you a break.

I wake up in the BRI,
At least I'm warm and fed
Perhaps it's a favour that they did me
At least I've got a bed.

There's more thugs on the outside
Then you'll ever meet within.
Prison's the tip of the iceberg
It's the streets that house the sin.

Anon

When You Left

You chipped away my confidence
You robbed me of my pride
You drained me of emotion
Yet when you left I cried.

I trusted you completely
Even though I know you lied
You wrapped me round your finger
And when you left you cried

My world came down around me
'Cos it's on you that I relied
I'll never give my heart again
Because when you left it died.

Anon

High-Rise Blues

Money's short and times are hard,
The icy cold wind bites.
In high-rise flats we build our homes,
Next door to building sites.
A urine-sodden coffin takes us to our floors
The syringes and the rubbish,
Build up at our doors.
Out of sight and out of mind,
Nobody seems to care.
The muggers hide in shadows,
To catch you unaware.
Single mums above me,
Dealers down below.
A rotting stench around me,
The way out I don't know.

Anon *(Horfield Prison)*